Edge of the Echo

Edge of the Echo

Poems

KB Ballentine

Iris Press
Oak Ridge, Tennessee

Cover Photo: Pavel Kašák

Book Design: Robert B. Cumming, Jr.

Iris Press
www.irisbooks.com

Library of Congress Cataloging-in-Publication Data

Names: Ballentine, KB, author.
Title: Edge of the echo : poems / KB Ballentine.
Identifiers: LCCN 2021002370 (print) | LCCN 2021002371 (ebook) | ISBN 9781604542646 (paperback) | ISBN 9781604548174 (ebook)
Subjects: LCGFT: Poetry.
Classification: LCC PS3602.A6218 E34 2021 (print) | LCC PS3602.A6218 (ebook) | DDC 811/.6—dc23
LC record available at https://lccn.loc.gov/2021002370
LC ebook record available at https://lccn.loc.gov/2021002371

Acknowledgements

20/20 Vision Scotland: "*Ard na Said*"
Abyss and Apex: "Ocean View"
American Diversity Report: "Beltane Blaze," "Born Into Legend," and "Edge of the Echo"
Amethyst Review: "Between Sky and Sea" and "In Praise of Oceans"
Atlanta Review: "Days of Blackbird"
Avocet: "Always the Wind," "Autumn's Lament," "Eight Questions," "Sight, Hindered," "Starlight Falling," "Taste of Shadows," and "Words, Circling"
Bindweed: "Living Like This"
Coffin Bell: "Darkness Has a Shape," "Dark Throat of Evening," and "Pursued"
Commonthought: "*Shomerim* at Birkenau"
Concīs: "The Morrigan Rides"
Delta Poetry Review: "Waiting for Winter" and "What Was Told"
Dissonance Magazine: "Bramble and Thorn"
Door Is A Jar: "To Know the Darkness"
Ekphrastic Review: "Masks"
Haight-Ashbury: "Permanence Has Nothing to Do With Love"
Halcyon Days: "Fall, Unleaving" and "Saturday Mornings"
It Matters Radio: "Scent of Autumn"
Jellyfish Whispers: "Written in Water"
Kind of a Hurricane: Emergence Anthology: "Thirteen Skeins"
Midnight Circus: "Fistful of Dirt" and "Pocket of Cinders"
Minute Magazine: "A Story Worth Telling"
Mountain Anthology: "Learning to Breathe"
Nightingale & Sparrow: "All Soul's Night"
Oyster River: "Released into the Blue"
Panoply: "Anatomy of a Ruin" and "The Whole Sky Wakes"
Parks and Points: "Rising Umber"
Peacock Journal: "Ardgroom," "Taste of Salt," and "Tree, Singing"
Plum Tree Tavern: "Ocean Triptych"

PoetryMagazine.com: "Blue, Ragged Wind" and "Fieldstone Grief"
Poetry Quarterly: "Edging Toward Dusk" and "The Gray Hour"
Poetry South: "The Burning of Flipper Bend" and "The Forgetfulness of Rain"
Pudding Magazine: "Borrow the Light" and "Words Dropped, Shining"
Quill and Parchment: "Invitation"
RHINO: "Ghost Garden"
Sequestrum: "Blood Summer," "Darkness Weaves the Hours," and "Gathering Dreams"
Sheila-na-Gig: "Aurora at Rest," "Let Your Hands Remember," and "Threading Time"
Sublunary Review: "Hunger of Wanting"
Trouvaille Review: "How the Rain Falls"
Weekly Avocet: "Blue Moon," "In Praise of Snow," and "Zen of Birds"
Wild Word: "At the Letting Go" and "Return My Dreams to Me"

I would be remiss not to thank the many people who continually help and support me in my work: Diane Frank, Helga Kidder, Chris Wood, Karen Slikker, David Austin, James Harrison, Jim Canestrari, and Buddy and Susan Ballentine. Several workshop groups and my Open Mic members provide useful insight and comments, and I appreciate their help as well. To my faithful readers: thank you. Receiving your emails and messages keep me going when I don't feel like working. You give me purpose and focus, and I appreciate you more than you'll ever know.

*Life is the fire that burns and the sun that gives light. Life is the wind
and the rain and the thunder in the sky. Life is matter and is earth,
what is and what is not, and what beyond is in Eternity.*

—Lucius Annaeus Seneca

Contents

Fire

Prologue

A Story Worth Telling

—Trinity Library, Dublin

Nibs and quill scratch vellum deep with ink
like the point of a spear, a hawk gripping cliff tops.
Permanent loops and blots feather Amergin's words,
seal them into scrolls unsung—
unwound seven times seven generations later.
Letters shaping into language ripple like ocean waves
spilling into dark and whispered rooms: Listen.

Space Between Bones

Weathered stone stretches the Burren—
pleats and pockets where wild thyme and bloody cranesbill
struggle past the lime, the rain
to perforate the moonscape.

I never tire of this: waves worrying the shingle,
pipits and wheatear chittering, parachuting the sky,
cuckoos crying from a hedgerow.

Wind claims my weariness as I breathe
the gloaming, the brine, the fire of ice-white stars,
the sod. This is what stays.

Air

*Source of the breath
that enables flowers to flourish,
and calls the dark-rooted trees
to ascend into blossom.*

—John O'Donohue

Relentless as Breathing

I am seafoam, I am star,
            light and dark.
        I am the purpling of redbud trees,
the butterscotch of falling leaves,
                shadow of the solstice night.
        Above, around, inside me
heaven beckons—dawn's pink sky,
                bluebirds soaking, ruffling a puddle.
                Each day the wind, the sun
    urge me on, this spinning sapphire
sphere circling a saffron sun.
                Red tips of a blackbird, an oriole,
the violet deep in wrinkling dusk,
        the cold stream surprising a mountain gap
                sing something greater than we know,
nothing less than what we are.

Thin as Air

—Dingle, Ireland

Memory weights this place, this island,
with images of you: Atlantic flooding
the shingled beach as you race the tide,
twilight crouching behind the Three Sisters
where you and wind cling to the cliffs.
Día dhuit and *Día is Muire dhuit* in the pub—
sláinte and laughter before anger rends the air
and glass shatters, shards the smooth-planked floor.

How do I go back again? Hay meadows
just beginning to bud with buttercups,
hares hiding in timothy and quaking grass.
Green hills, fields still tumbling into the ocean,
shearwaters skating its rumpled surface.
Mist rising, erasing   you   bit by   bit.

One Thing I Have Learned

In country light we walk back slow
—where we once lived and loved.
—Al Young

When you wake and the dream still sings,
       when fireside strokes warmth into your bones,
when vapor licks the river, kisses your cheek with mist,
       when wren and bluebird dwell in the curve of hickory
and stars pulse the moon's heartbeat—
       know you are in my marrow, in my soul.

No stranger to loss,
       shadows of the Fall still sizzle
the gloom, just out of sight.
       Truth thirsts for happiness, gnaws
       the edge of grief until you surrender—
              let memory drift

to that kitchen table where mama and aunts weave gossip,
       and love tastes like fried chicken, perfumed hugs,
or like the first tug of your son's fingers,
       or even following dad's faltering steps
across ammonia-scented rooms.

Knowing this will hurt
       but risking it anyway.

More than a muscle, the heart
       breathes, leaving nothing behind.

A Taste of Shadow

Brambled gloom puckers the path
as I walk home, moon climbing the hill
ahead of me. A fox yips, echoes
in the valley, and something shifts in the laurel,
skitters away. Cold air strokes my throat
while I hum *I'll give you a daisy a day, dear,*
and the porch light beckons,
sweeping away lingering darkness.
Your shadow swallows the open door—
and the four winds we know blow away…

The Gray Hour

The night watch lengthens—
cat's paws stalk the pond,
and wind groans through the ash groves,
cedars singing under a burning moon.

Crickets sigh beneath bloodroot
sparking the darkness,
and the bones of the nightingale tingle
like ink scratched onto a blank page, bare flesh—
broken shadows revealing the woodline.

The day's rage bellows,
lopes into the void
while sleep struggles, hesitates.
Twilight interrogates the ebony sky,
stars whispering into mist,
roses kissing the horizon.

What If?

Sickle moon slices, clouds score the sky.
Fog blinds the valley, and silence circles,
chains us to our thoughts.
Mired in yesterday we choke,
wonder if we could have made a difference.
Stars struggle beyond the mist,
beyond what's left of our dreams.

To Know the Darkness

Plumped with cold, bluebirds haunt
the hickories—branches scratching the white sky.
A breeze brisks fallen leaves, dried
and fracturing into loam. The rhythm
of winter has locked us in place,
grim stirrings of frost and flake growling
in clouds gray and frozen over the horizon:
crows fenced on poles—
inked silhouettes of the coming night.

Darkness Has a Shape

Demon, demon, you have dumped me

like Sylvia's daddy into red poppies
that blister my skin, settle into my heart

Nobody cared if the moon went black
when he shrugged and walked away

The trees groaned as he passed,
wrens winging through shifting leaves

Each knows where the others are

When doubt clutches the belly, the brain
refuses to play its part

An actor on strike, nothing to say
lines lost or broken, tumbled

into the darkness of yesterday
falling away from tomorrow

where everything is only waiting

Days of Blackbird

Frost furs the spruce, the pine, needles
shivering under nebulous starlight.
Branches dolloped like milkbloom
stretch into these dark nights of no moon.
Imbolc awaits.
Shadows fist the boxwood
where blackbirds gabble: *hurry, hurry, hurry.*
Midnight sweeps icy wings as snowdust echoes
the silent stars—falling,
                              falling.

Blue, Ragged Wind

—for a student

Sky stunned by the news—
                you will not be back.
          I stare into the blue, atoms dissolving,
      taking away the shape of you.

Absorbed into Bryant's earthly coach,
          into Donne's wakeful eternity,
             you have traveled a distance we cannot
        reach. Robbed from us
     the young man we knew.

No noon sun can warm us from this cold
           rumor. No night more chilling
        than today's dawn, when a dragonfly darted
      over the lake, the sky, in lonely flight,
          light broken and scattered behind.

Always the Wind

February sobs a chiffon frost,
morning sky like parchment, bone.
Bits of star, snow float like cottonwood,
shiver in porcelain air.
And the voice of the mountain summons,
my heart thumping its slow dirge.

A stream—ice lacing edges—
spatters the rocks, leaps
and plunges again to alabaster ground.
The fringe of winter circles us,
spring's pearl swelling the belly of earth.

Zen of Birds

If I got to choose another life
    a closer, meaner life
        a simpler, more focused life
        I'd like to be a bird—

a cardinal shrub-bright in February rain
    a bluebird fluffing feathers, puddle-bathing
        a hawk skimming July thermals
river shrinking and swelling below.

    Meaty meals of gnats and flies
        worms and grubs, reaping seed
            from backyard feeders, winging
    through studded branches, green leaves—

not a crow ghosting the oak
    but a wren, plain and small
        psalming the dawn.

What was Told

—after Rumi

to the cornflower sky as clouds scribbled by?
What was told to the bluebird as it tousled
feathers in a lazy puddle? Does the perfume
in a hawthorn stem sing to a green spring day?
Does the oak swaying toward the maple whisper
a welcome, a husky *how are you today?*
What was told to the twilight as the firefly sparked
or to the cosmos as a bee kissed its silky center?
What was told the morning you were born,
after the pain and the sweat and the tears—
that my heart could shatter and still be made whole.

Blue Moon

Arctic ocean dissolves into indigo clarity,
March sky still brittle with star and ice.
Peacocks dream blueberries and azure lakes,
though cornflowers, robin eggs blink through frost.
The turquoise world yawns,
cobalt and lapis flickering in the depths—
Little Boy Blue inks my veins,
faint jazz notes, sax tapping my jeans,
bluebirds winging north, tasting spring.

Threading Time

More than broken stars,
our vapor sketches the sky—
bits of crystal, of ice burning the night.
Filmed in negative, a trail of ravens gliding by.
Pine distilled to turpentine slips through furrowed bark,
hawthorn flowering, fruiting then rotting in heat and frost.

Wind chronicles our change,
our trek beyond the ash grove to stone circles
that silhouette ever-greening fields leaning
into the sea. Waves salt the rock, the sand
with a breath of what's left of us.
A grain. Just one—hungering for more.

Turning, of a Wheel

Midsummer moon slips over the horizon,
  stars still dreaming behind their clouds.

    Rain barrel full, furrows flood, pucker and soften to
      mud.
      Veined canvases, the leaves shiver, droplets
        tumbling.

        Forest floor sketched with sassafras and hickory,
          branches groan as a moonbow curves the sky.

         Sea-holly sleeps in shadows,
         blue petals mingling with midnight.

         Waves froth and fizz, sands pulsing
       with starfish. Spray scatters, salts rock and cliff.

      Ravens wrestle in the blackthorn, barbs slicing the
       air.
  A vixen yips, darkness echoing.

  Eyes wide, an owl blinks between the rowan trees.
Night of the faeries. Lock your doors.

The Morrigan Rides

Caul of night invades the Black Valley,
   crow roams the still-warm thermals,
Gap of Dunloe stained red with stonecrop.
   Dundee masked beneath MacGillycuddy's Reeks,
Coosaun Lough slips low, Wishing Bridge creaking,
   groaning as doves keen in the pilings.
Blackthorn spikes horizon's fire, an owl swiveling
   its neck, eyes wide at the coming dark.

Bramble and Thorn

Cows, brindled in shade and sun,
blur the ridge—bassoon of frogs
and woodline chandeliered by green.
Warblers thread the sky where clouds wisp,
bees gyrating over the last lace-caps,
hydrangea blue now seared with autumn.

Leathered language strafes the air waves,
debates battering my ears, my breath.
My thoughts bleeding (still bleeding).
Across the field a hay baler snarls,
and somewhere up north a boy slashes his arm
with a buzz-saw. Harvest demands a sacrifice.

Tonight meteors will shower our wishes
through galaxies we cannot see.
Rain turned red on some other planet falling,
still falling.

All Soul's Night

The veil thins… shreds. The dead
     and living will mingle this night.
Light shrivels, shadows staking claims.
       Sea grumbles in the distance, air surging
salt and winter, gulls quarreling
      their way home.
Inland, crabapples wither where they fall,
      a few leathered leaves hinged
               to baring braches.

No black cats, specters or formless mist
      will keep me in tonight—too long
since I last breathed you.

Between Soft Shadows

Mist as thin as faerie wings
slips over my skin, day wrapping
itself in cotton-fog. Yesterday's muzzy sun
lured us with its summer warmth—
just enough blue to make a pair of pants,
and an ocean kissed with salt and sand.
But a cold wind drifted in,
now spider lace trembles with wet worlds.

A damselfly hums somewhere.
Trust the faeries to share their grace
as I walk into this day unknowing.
Let water leap and curl the shore.
Let gray blur scatter
into specks of breath—a faerie brushing by.

Learning to Breathe Again

—Cairngorm Mountains, Scotland

The Cairngorms yawn into dawn,
ribbons of fog weaving
above rounded peaks.

Sun saturates mist, light dissolving
echoes from the past—
the shadow, the blur.

Memory and atoms coalesce—
water lilies pause,
a butterfly punctures the breeze,
you stab my thoughts.

The River Spey wrinkles south
where gorse, heather bristle together.

Oh, the beauty, the sting.

Masks

I dream olive trees as rain pings glass,
veins windows in swirling tapers,
remembering the heat of Greece, you.

Gnarled branches offered scraps of shade,
Ionian Sea too far for fondling breeze
under blue sky burning.

I discovered you there, where all roots dive deep.
Marketplace stacked with cobblestone,
woven blankets, pottery fired and glazed
like grandfather's grandfather shaped.

You hovered like a butterfly, Eros's breath
searing my shoulder, nibbling the nectar of my lips,
fingers like wings brushing skin.

But somewhere across the ocean,
past frosted caribou-crossed land,
you withdrew. Psyche lures, and you listen
to voices from the past, sputter with doubt, fear.

Oh, *petalouda*, which is the real you?

Words, Circling

To make my poems surge and sing
I would kidnap the color and chorus of birds.

I'd seize the bright flash of bluebird
that combines sky, hydrangeas, summer sea
and mix it with the wren's sun-bronzed song.

I would catch the language of sorrow
and love that weave through each line
of a thrush's melody, the harmony of the finch
burnishing stanza's timbre.

Hijack nuthatch and meadowlark to pry deep
into the verse of trees,
flies and gnats snatched mid-air.

Let passion blaze like a cardinal's fire in winter nests
when couplets, tercets collide.

The shimmery pulse of hummingbirds capture cadence,
sweetness and luster so small,
discovered only by tender readers.

Circling above, blackbird inks words with a silent turn
of curved head, listening to the rhythm, the shade, the echo

of tears.

Words Dropped, Shining

You hide on my porch, wait
until I brew tea and bring cream
to the table. You scorn all candles
except patchouli—musk and moss slipping
into the air, bees clinging to the screen,
wrens brushing close. You like the restlessness
of the nuthatch, the cardinals as they hop
from one feeder to the next.

Steam drifts from the pot as I pour a cup,
let it heal my somnolence.
All morning you embrace, refresh me,
and ink surges across the page—
but you wane as the sun slides high, higher,
moths brushing by, and then you're gone.
Cup and saucer smudged and stained,
notebook crowded with scribbles and blots.

Promise to meet me tomorrow.

Name the darkness

where towhee and cedar waxwing sing promises
from the birch, the beech.
Goose Creek stirs as dusky dawn purples
then blushes the sky.

Night crawled with questions, stalked
my sleeplessness.
Roaming the rooms, thoughts thorning
my brain, I witnessed mist slide in,
a robe that should welcome, not reject, sleep.

When wind roused the white threads,
brushed them into nothingness,
a ceiling of stars crossed the heavens,
moon slivered and dim.

And now the wren, the chickadee shift,
open their throats to the new day.
Doubts still unanswered but drifting with the dark,
a faint rumor dissolving in echoes of light.

Eight Questions

—after Maurice Manning

Who decides how many times the earth will loop
the sun, when an eclipse will devour the moon?
How does a raindrop balance from a holly berry,
a new leaf, the tip of my lover's nose?
Why do crows crowd in sevens—one for each day
of creation plus a rest? How do the deer know
the hinge of night, trust twilight's fading: to blend
into a field of grass, the grass dissolve into earth,
the earth pulverize and polish seeds of salt to feed the deer?
Does a dolphin sing to itself? Why do I shiver
when you tease my flesh, my skin smolder under your touch?
How can a dragonfly's translucent wings, the stubby body
of the lumbering bumble bee ride the wind? Upon my soul,
how do chimes in a summer breeze dance a tune called *home*?

Earth

Let us salute the silence
and certainty of mountains:
their sublime stillness,
their dream-filled hearts.

—John O'Donohue

Ardgroom Stone Circle

How many thousands of years have you been there?
—Ho Xuan Huong

Bark wet with rain, the hemlock drips,
shards of liquid carving valleys
into the trunk. Echoing fissures in rock,
layers of gray marbling the hills.

Through tufts of grass, creeping jenny flickers
and still the stones wait. Fog and dew web
the meadow, the small cairn in the center.
Ragged path rings the circle, fixed and frozen.

Feet, legs damp from the walk-about, I pause.
Kittiwakes cry overhead. Ocean shushes the shore
where chamomile and cats-ear cling
in Kenmare Bay.
                    Salt scatters, tickles
my lips, my tongue. Blue rushes stretch and blur
the horizon. Starlings shift shadows,
argue in hedgerows. *Who was here first?*

A gust ruffles my hair, surges past
and I head for home. Clouds scoot east,
scraps of stars faint and far above.
Traces of gold, lavender on the rim of night.

Through the Sod

Follow the stony path to Caherconnell—
firepit cold and ashless, wind colder still
as it breaks, blows through the gaps,
taps my spine. Rain spits
and the chill persists, though it's June.
Calves nose for water, for grass in a farmer's field.
Waves of green erode into gray on slate gray.

Spades shape the rock, the dirt—
archaeologists pursuing the past
in bits of chert, of clay.
They brush away layers of today,
hooded crows circle silently,
watch from the hedgerows.
Secrets safe and silent as your grave.

Edging Toward Dusk

Clouds kneel over the mountain,
gray upon gray bowed.
Leaves freckle in the forgiving light,
November not yet piercing—
pursuing the dead, the dying.

The blue coolness of spring too far away,
I shiver as geese ghost the sky, a heron
gulps the last bit of fish.
Accept these days as we lean,
as we stumble from the light.

Living Like This

—in Ireland's West Country

The swans are gone from Coole Park,
the corncrakes from Shannon's banks.
Gorse tumbles the hillside to the river's edge,
but Yeats's *nation of believers* no longer kneels or even prays.
Rain hides scars chafing under the damp, under the thorns.
Reflected sunset washes coral and sky-blue houses.
Broken slate, sagging thatch buckles under this need
to snag everything before it rushes past.

Music riddles the pubs in a fusion of Arabic, Indian, and French—
Johnny Cash with a twist, but *Pour me another, Liam*
ricochets the night. Rent is due, and the lights blink
out one by one by one, gorse gleaming in the dusk.
What's left of the peat crumbles into incense,
an offering of sorts.

Tree, Singing

—after Wallace Stevens

One must have a mind of trees
        to frisk in summer breezes, dip limbs
    in time to the rhythm of the wind,

    and have been warmed by August sun
to shift and burn, to smolder in October's gold,
            copper, crimson flames.

To cradle nesting squirrels curled around a heap
        of nutty sweetness and the scratch of owl's talon-grip
when frosts lace scarred and withered bark.

        Cardinal-fire balanced on needle branches
snagged with snow, white weight bending
        till it strokes the blinded earth.

When green peeks, sneaks through gray-brown husks
        and harmonies, melodies flutter between our leaves,
    we breathe the Lenten rose and bloodroot far below,

believe in everything again.

At the Letting Go

Cranes strut, swagger across the sandy flatland.
By the hundreds they lurch, searching for roots, for grain.
Soon they will rise, sky full of fury and then—
silence, a blankness in the blue, blue canvas.

In another season, pomegranates plump.
Red-orange buds trumpet into tart-tongued globes.
Trees bow with heavy treasure, and juice seeps,
ferments until a withered mass browns,
sags through thorns onto parched grass.

And you, my dear, you stagger toward excuses,
grasp as high as you can.
Fingertips caressing the skin, you lose
your balance.   Fall.

Field Stone Grief

Memory swarms—promises sown,
flown like thistle, like flies.
Scattered to who knows where.
Days patterned like gray tile, like slate
hanging heavy from the sky, my heart.
Not even a breath flows through
the fissures, splinters shorn and sharp.
Crows hover, shadow the yard.
They watch me watching and do not blink.

Sight, Hindered

Cut grass and hay suffuse the sky
with beads of pollen, seed.
Galway blinks, a sheen of mist lingering.
Longing.
Late spring and lambs leap in fields
where daisies surprise, mesmerize me—
grasping, my hand learns weeds.
Hydrangeas sigh blush and blue,
heirlooms of summer.
Next year at this time buds and leaves will pulse,
last year's bloom faded, forgotten.
I'm still searching for the house of belonging,
for a light by which to see.
Lone oak shivers in the breeze, whispers,
Where are you today?
Hooded crow *caw, caws* at cousin magpie,
skims the strand to hug woodline, hedgerows
that swallow his shadow.
The melody of wrens, thrushes make me ache,
storm clouds shifting, blurring the horizon.

A Fistful of Dirt

Blackthorn braids the fen, peat stacked
like brick, smudged stars rippling into vapor.
Dawn devours the sky. *How long
will you weary my thoughts?*

Clouds riot the west, and spring tiptoes closer.
Purple-veined speedwell pulses
through snowfall clinging like bog cotton,
furrowed field still frozen, stiff as bone.

Heart captured, my lips refuse the silence,
sigh your name as the quarter moon sinks
with your memory under a swelling tide of blue.
Underground, palaces of root scar the darkness.

The Hollow Hill

Follow the ash and elm wood
until you discover the clearing,
the field that rises into a mound
where a solitary hawthorn reigns.
October frosts the sky blue.

The forest behind you waits.
Branches scratch, hooded crows
caw, caw—scatter your thoughts.
The wind curls around you, tugs
your hair as a lover might.

Day passes. The sun mellows
into gold, spins pink and orange
into ether as fiddles,
hornpipes, bodhráns shape
a melody that lulls your senses.

You stare at the hawthorn, at the hill
where it stands. A sickle moon knifes
the twilight. Stars glint but vanish
in growing mist. Light smolders
then glows as the music swells.

A barn owl shrieks past.
Field, forest empty.

Permanence Has Nothing to Do With Love

Stones tumble from collapsing fences.
Ivy spills the gaps, loops and reddens
as Fall follows fast—
stars pearling the long dark night.
From the sea a salt breeze stirs, storms
the shore in a surge of spray—
cold, colder.

Across the cove, a neighbor's candle flicks
the darkness, licks their window with light,
moon a sharp groove in the heavens.
Anyplace we love becomes our world.
That world is you. Sheets snap on the line—
ghosts abandoned to the shadows.
Winter encroaching.

Let Your Hands Remember

—Digging in Tully West, Kildare, Ireland

Wind complains, shivers each branch overhanging the site—
boxed and numbered, a register of time from stone and peat:

bowls of promise, full of wheat or coin, lavender or wyrt.

Trace the painted wings—
glaze cracked, dancing, skirting the lip and belly.

Shaved clay flakes, ridges engraved
with the potter's prints, voice baked
in fire and steam singing,   still singing.

Mead Moon rising, a chalked horse glints on the hill
as honeyed notes of the wren echo in the hedgerow.

Life interrupted—caught between then and now
as sunset searches the leaves, the earth for more.

Forgetfulness of Rain

Rain echoes in my dreams—
        drizzling hush that shifts
                into syncopated downpour.

I wake to sun-split clouds,
leaves that crackle and whirl
into faerie winds and frisk
down the road, quelled
only by the dying breeze,
the rising heat this November.

Thunder grumbles
then withers into distance
and patterns each day until we weary
of ourselves, our thoughts
shriveling like the azaleas,
the hostas not bothering to bloom.
Even the raspberries yield only thorns.

Squirrels nudge acorn husks,
consider the leftover birdseed.
Ravens shadow the back deck,
and the nuthatch spirals down
the bark of the blackgum until I'm dizzy
with longing, my hands empty.

        My heart waits the promise of rain…
                of faeries… of sustenance—anything
                        but this bleak winter desert.

At What Cost?

—Dunmurry, Ireland, 1978

Bulldozers halt at meadow's edge.
Pilgrims push past the barricade,
mourn the strips of cloth, photos, letters
hanging from broken branches
                    dragging the dust.

Curses and laments stain the air,
despair raining this gray day.
Road crews retreat from the prodding
mob, and crows protest overhead.

Prayers echo as penitents circle
the hawthorn, whispers crossing the fractured field.
Scrim of night lowering,
the foreman orders his workers, everyone home.

Dusk ripples, pleats the sky
a painter's periwinkle and silence shivers.
Faerie lights blink and sputter,
                  fade from the shattered tree.

Hunger of Wanting

Silence widens, snow pausing
   like an archer, breath suspended,
as a stag grazes into the meadow.
     Numb, the stars witness all.
    In this Moon after Yule twilight,
flakes drift into crevices, downy piles
      soft as cat fur as they first cover my feet
then gather faster, stalking the darkness
   with feather-light.
     I peer into shadows for you, hesitate
like a wolf surprising scent, snow
   muffling any cries.

Haibun for Auvillar, France

The journey from Old Town to New is no great distance, but the hills are steep and take longer than I expect. Passing narrow alleyways where shadows can't shroud graffiti from sand-colored stone, rotten cherries stink the sky. Clotted cotton rolls across the blue, pebbles pierce my feet. A reminder to pilgrims the way is not easy even when lined with Ronsard roses. Figs ripen behind wrought iron, but the river unfurls below.

Thick with memories—
paper and sorrow stitch her
wide and grasping mouth

Seeding Darkness

The leaf has a song in it.
—Mary Oliver

Each studded branch unfists its green,
shadows swallowed in lengthening light.
The hinge of spring lifts, song echoing
in the growing things: milk and sap,
egg and bud—a meditation of days
as they unfold…

my moments spent breathing
this new season—
the cruelest month, with sweet showers,
a spirit of youth, full of whispers
and tonight's starshine all are true.
Each day a different key:
the locks, the notes alter,
and we must be ready to lift our voices
whatever may come.
                Whatever comes.

Ard-na-Said

—Height of the Arrows, Edinburgh, Scotland

Sky sheds its blue, clouds sighing
across the cliff's shoulder. We trudge under hazel trees
that guard the lower fields, edges puckered
with thistle and nettle. Slope etched now by trails,
tracks of ice-scars and pillow lava brood
just beneath the grass. Cocooned in leaf and bramble,
sedge and willow warblers carol in horse-tail ferns, in rowan.

From the ridge, the Firth of Forth laments
the shore, castle and city stretching west,
highlands crouched in the east. Sun and shadow
haggle as rain-light strokes the horizon.
Here we fling our wishes, our sorrows—
wind plucking each word, each hope coaxed
from our lips, promising nothing.

Anatomy of a Ruin

—Elgin Cathedral, Scotland

Starlings scuffle above gabled doorway
      gaping to fen and field.   Imagine a soft click
            and the wide wood door unlatches,
                              swings open
   to yawning gray,
            Mary invisible in dusky corners.

            But it's just the sky,
                              a bundle of mist
      that sheens the stone,   lancet windows spearing,
echoing two towers as they climb,
                        eclipse the gravestones.
            The abbey chants its secrets,
                  hints of straw, wine, sandalwood whisper the air.
   Gold fades, veins remaining ceiling,
         cobwebs wisping columns, crevices.
The river curves its melody to the coast,
                        a crescendoing capriccio
         surging into the sea.

   Wolves have tracked the moors,
                  snarl outside these crumbling walls.
         Light flickers in the Lantern of the North,
                              where shadows   stretch
         under
                  a rioting moon.

Emptiness Where Song Should Be

Driving through Irish villages, fens and folds
shift, the color of cinnamon brandy and marsh green
where bog cotton bemuses the pure air.
Sky still blue, rain promises—
thunder clouds like ivory towers.
Horizon embraces shore and mountain,
blackthorns ancient, copper beeches split and gnarled.

Back home, a weary version of itself
gazes through infinity mirrors.
Architects with one good design to build again and again—
a plague of suburbs.
Some invisible line drawn
across the neighborhoods where no one plays
outside at noon. House swallows and gold finches
flicker the empty spaces—a protest
to the silence, a complaint for drained and nameless days.

Rising Umber

—Grimspound, Dartmoor National Park, England

Dusk lavenders the horizon,
and in the half-light
the stones begin to speak.
Wind slips across the mountain,
asterisks of mist softening the ruins.

Sheep drift through the field,
tufts of green hollowed into havens
for leggy lambs.
I cross the collapsing threshold
beside a wall still stacked,
still circling crumbled huts.

A ram eyes me, shambles to his hooves
and paws the grass.
Swallowtails rush, scythe the air,
hooded crow stalking the shadows.
I stoop into the shelter of stones
where wind fades,
palpable stillness rioting the air.

Through gathering gloom, a man and woman emerge
crossing the ridge of stone—
They scan the valley, silhouettes bruising,
ghosting the ribbons of fog.

When I glance again only emptiness,
star-breath, slivered moon paling the sky.
An owl summoning the dark.

Almost-Death in Ballymena

The afternoon was closing fast, and we were headed back.
Passing fields and cows and trees had lured us quite off-track.
While village greens and cobbled streets wove their magic
    charms,
we laughed and snacked and photographed and glimpsed the
    greening farms.
We travelled on a city road we thought would be a breeze—
a wider lane, clearer signs, and lots of pubs to please.
A side-street tour, two curved roads: our hearts skipped then
    quickly dropped.
Traffic lights flashed red *and* green—we jolted to a stop.
Staring through the windshield, we wished we'd not been born,
now nose-to-nose with a vintage car that beeped its tinny horn.
We spun the wheel then backed away and fled the asphalt arena,
and when the sun ducked below the trees, we were far from
    Ballymena.

Scent of Autumn

Sky scored with rain,
Wine Moon simmers behind clouds,
an owl staining the night.

Apples plump branches
as gnarled as a witch's hand.

Like lightning raking the sky,
an unkindness of ravens bites—
rush of wings choking the crickets' sigh.

Summer's cadence crescendos into silence.
Weeds scratch against hickory, sassafras,
golden arms stretched against the fitful light.

Fire

To be loved means to be consumed in the flame;
to love is to shine with inexhaustible light.

—John O'Donohue

Festival of Fire

Amber shadows seal day's fate,
soften the lines of the foothills.
Along its base, bonfires glitter
through the valley, shouts and laughter
sing the air as bodhráns throb
a rhythm of spring's ending.

In a larceny of nectar, bees hum home,
and fireflies flicker, take their place.
Darkness devours remnants of light,
and mist swirls across stars flaring the sky.

The Comfort of Solitude

Night lingers.
A silver-spotted skipper skims the window
where my lamp beckons—a tiny sun.
Moth moon cradles the cedars,
branches stroking dawn's purple skirt.
The crickets' cadence, the dove's sad song wane,
pink fingers spreading the sky—
light discovers a fawn, a splintered swing.
Morning's heartbeat a mystery
unfolding as stars dissolve,
a mockingbird flirting with fallen figs…

Aurora at Rest

Nightmares can't scorch her sleep—
only dissolve as stars spin,
ring the universe. Slivers of dreams
coalesce, gathering strength and light
though silence and shadow surround her.
Color swells and explodes,
and even the darkness cannot consume her.

She doesn't see it yet, but veins of promise
pulse, sequin the galaxy. Sunbursts surge and spiral.
Like a phoenix, she wakes, blazes with life.

Beltane Blaze

Dawn blossoms May's moon,
tempts white-winged moths
to worship the dew.

The widow of Coomcallee limps
the riverbank, seeks the shallows,
water shushing pebble, stone.

She scatters primrose and violet
while sun mounts the blue, rowan and hawthorn
shivering with faerie breath.

A kestrel cries
over the chatter of ash branches.

Two men urge cows into fields
between stacked wood,
and village girls curtsy the maypole.

Candles balance on windowsills,
tempting the flames of this night.

Come to the fire when the mist
closes in, sing and shout and dance.

Don't look far into the dark,
just hold out your hand to ward off the stars
and believe the morning will win.

The Whole Sky Wakes

Fireflies, frogs sing in summer heat—
last gasp before blackgum and oaks groan
in October mist. Figs wither
and fall, twilight's shroud dusted with pine.

Veining the sky in silver, lightning
slips south. A sudden silence disturbs
evening's chorus, hints of jasmine
drifting, dazzling the night.

Clouds shield the stars, muting
the voice of the moon. She pauses,
halo wavering, pulsing. Pursues
kisses among fading starshine.

Saturday Mornings

—after Denton Loving

I like the way your body warms the morning,
sheets a nest of softness and scent.
How sunrise infuses the blinds,
the curtains, wraps us in golden light.
The ticking of your watch and the heater's grumble
the only sounds beneath our sleepy murmurs.
Photos grin from the dresser,
dust dancing in swelling brightness.
Your pajama pants worn and nubby under my hand,
the coffee maker beeps, almond roast luring
us from bed. Together we smooth the pillows,
the comforter. I make scones while you build a fire,
cherry wood, hickory beginning to flame,
to heat the room, me—as you have.

Awake a Fire

The fire burning earth's heart howls,
sizzles through veins of clay and dirt,
        roaming with flickering fingers
the belly of this world.
    Tongues of sulphur herded
into geysers deny the sky its stars
while lightning sears ephemeral darkness.
        Hearths smoored until morning, ashes wrap
the bright berry of flame,
        spared another night to crowd this home
with warmth and light. Sealed beneath our feet,
it dances—the earth throbs and shivers.

Blood Summer

Ruby throat pulsing,
a hummingbird fevers the air,
pulls nectar from crimson columbine,
tomatoes plumping on the vine.

July sparks on a San Francisco pier,
sears a Chattanooga parking lot, a Lafayette theater—
hearts and sirens bleeding,
Mars hanging heavy overhead.

Night gathers and fury flares
like fireworks—
brake lights blazing bright—
chipped brick, vivid lips, spilled wine.

But no one on the red-eye spots
the thermometer's boiling bulb,
cherries bursting their stems—
sun burning the sky like red-hot coals.

Shomerim at Birkenau

Tagged with the numbers scarred
on my grandmother's arm, I step through
the open gate once barred against her.

Crass browns assail scarlet and gold,
the treasure of trees condemned to scatter
paths, to be raked and burned in piles.

North winds seize summer's moisture, dawn
and dusk drier, colder. Sky crouches closer,
buildings lean in, cling to earth.

A fly frisks my face, lone reminder of the swarms
these fields once fueled. Concrete walls chill
afternoon heat, tourists bumping the tight spaces.

Blackened ovens crumble into dirt,
rust staining ash. Voices from the past
and present mingle, whisper together the Kaddish.

Ghost Garden

I keep having this dream that there is a garden
growing inside my chest, under the bones.
—Melissa Studdard

I dream of the bunks at Ravensbrück
where lice writhe soft and fat, as white as lilies
across the skin, across the scalp

    Remember your little garden where musk roses
    blushed in May's cloudless sky
                 Ah, Moissac

The sky spits ash here
Lips, toes and fingers like pale blue orchids,
gnarled with cold, with cramp

    And what about the crocus,
    shoots peeking above the winter snow
                 Oh, Olesko

Dogs and cats vanished, the rats,
like purple pustules of irises
scratch the dirt, emerge

    Fields of poppies, blood-
    red blossoms free from the plow
                 Just so, Osjaków

Under the stone, under the bone
a violet sprouts   From your lungs,
her heart, buds of hyacinth

    I dream of bunks and pits and stench,
    guns and gas, hollow stomachs and souls—
        laughter unlearned, nights that last and last
and last

Darkness Weaves the Hours

When Orpheus rushed from darkness—
heart of fire left underground—
did crisp scents of scattered violets
or the rustling crunch of maple leaves shatter his senses?
Were stalks of green merging with moon orchids,
pink centers veining, staining pure petals?
Or were leather-barks of oaks peeling, breathing the frost?
Did his eyes sketch spring's frivolous curls,
despair lurching through bird song and sun,
or did he emerge into sighing mist
as it traced his own lost dreams?

Nerves pulsing swift and fierce at his neck
he risked the blackness, the coal, the ever-narrowing
tunnel that shrouded his body, sapped his will.
But when he saw her—oh, Eurydice!
the form of summer, all brightness and light—
silica glittered with crystals, roots curved into crowns.

Lily-skin hand he gripped,
plucked her through the mole-trapped rocks.
Gray-iron growls shook the hollows,
the gaps, the path.
Laughter of metal striking metal
deep in earth's dim core.

When Orpheus stumbled out of the sulphurous darkness—
fire of his heart left underground—
did her scream shudder the stone walls?
Does the echo keep him awake,
strings of a harp raveling… unraveling,
as he counts the stars
                    she cannot, will not see?

Summer Solstice Promise

Mountains shift as mist ghosts
    the ridge, spools the river.
Heat licks the sky, velvet-shirred,
    atoms cracking, dividing
right before our eyes. In the valley,
    heartwood trembles.
Fireflies flare the dusty road, blinking
    hope in this unfolding night.

The Burning of Flipper Bend

Smoke smothers the ridge,
chokes the gorge—97 days since rain
washed the creek beds, dusty tracks riddled
where clay shrinks and cracks.

Soddy Lake anchored in puddles,
banks scabbed, crusted with soot.
Blue herons, green light on the dock
blurred, no current to beat against—

Sky the hazy yellow of an air raid.
Houses and cars caked with pollen
from burning pine and thistle,
all that moves or stays masked—
ash of bird bone, a fox pup,
teeth still steaming from the heat.

Butterflies vanished—caterpillar sacs
morphed into blazing stars. Night sparks
with wings that will never fly.
Seeds dried and split, clouds secret,
somewhere far away, folding over a gray horizon
while we wait here, tongues parched, growing mute.

Dark Throat of Evening

The longest night seeps onto the horizon. Stillness
as tracks—squirrel? otter?—crystallize in the cold,
Oak Moon rising in a hungry sky.
A falcon dives, fur squirming, grasped in tight talons,
snow powdering the air.
Air sharp, stinging urges us through woods
where skeleton trees scratch the dusk,
limbs creak and snap.
The fox matches stride with the deer,
and ravens stalk hawthorn berries blood-red,
fiery against the pines. Darkness crouches close, swallows
winter's light and urges the candle, the fire,
the bolted the door.

Return My Dreams

You tasted like smoke and like trees.
I should have known you'd leave,
oh you'd leave—

But the hunger was worth the wait, worth the thorns.
I was already broken and bruised,
already torn.

Rain smudged the horizon the echo of sin,
your lips and your hands feasted
over my skin.

I breathed the sun and the stars for the very first time.
Strawberries in the park, flurried-snow surprise,
air singing like chimes.

Like nectar that drops from the hummingbird's beak,
we watched chicory purple and pulse
by the honeycombed creek.

Frogs in full chortle, spiders whispered their webs.
We laughed in a blossom-storm, honeysuckle and moss
fashioned the bed.

Darkness drowns your warmth, but a moon sparks the night.
Is it ok to the put my hand in the fire
if I can bring back the light?

Autumn's Lament

Husk of a sunflower sings autumn—
a tune that crackles with wind, with fire.
Sierra Nevada raging
until the pines, the aspens char
and sink with weight of coal and ash.

Storm and flood in Tennessee,
roses blushing in October drizzle.
Bluebirds fluff feathers.
Swing set and bicycles
beginning to rust.

And so the old year passes,
silver sickle swells to Harvest Moon—
light the candles, sweep the floors,
tomorrow's sorrow brushed
through yesterday's door.

Borrow the Light

The dream is always to be loved:
   fiery cardinals in February's drear,
warmth in winter shadows.
   Redbuds purpling the hillside,
green fields singing away snow.

   No one craves deserts or jungles—
scorching, steaming as sun and sweat blind
   what little we can see.
Or leaves marled red and gold choked
   into dull flakes that scuffle with the wind.

But each hour, each season scatters and harvests,
   weaves its own kind of love
so that each blue day becomes a blessing,
   night tiptoeing close,
but only so far.

Waiting for Winter

In these last days of root and branch,
of storms that stain maple and sassafras
with sunset and flame that summon the night—
seeds fall, nuzzle into mud, hearts pulsing
in darkness as the Blood Moon rises.
Butterflies frisk across chrysanthemums and asters,
honeyed dreams tempted and tasted.
Sunflowers crown browning fields,
hyssop peeking through thinning thickets.
Gold and purple sing visions of summer,
waning warmth humming with the wind.
Midnight lingers with a hush
as autumn tiptoes close, closer.

Pocket of Cinders

Anchored in gray, January spools
like quicksilver under the ashen sun.
Mice curl in curves, hollows of roots,
while mist hazes the lake.
The day waits. Slate.

Charcoaled on the horizon, mountains kiss
the graphite sky. Snow hesitates,
falls in fits—fresh frosting
on pewter powder already heaped
beside the road, asphalt and grit
crumbling in the cold.

Fall, Unleaving

Twilight surrenders, and an owl invites
us to savor the Dark Moon,
to explore shadow and light in negative form.
Peel away sight and we listen—
branches groan, dry leaves scratch
the yard with the same wind
that strokes our faces.
A wood fire smolders in a neighbor's hearth,
disguises the earth's loamy scent.
Snowflakes scatter, our tongues turning them to dew.
We wait as clouds shudder the sky.
Midnight approaches.
Ravens conspire, beg us to follow.   And we do.

Gathering Dreams for Sleep

—Les Canadiens by Cheryl Fortier

Light lazes the lake.
      Canoes, abandoned,
drift by the shore, red paint peeling
          onto lapping wavelets.
Maples glaze the mirrored surface,
      melody of sun and shadow laughing
         across water. Echoes of summer dance
    with dragonflies, the last bee.
Butternut sweetens the air,
        darkness falling faster as a cardinal
   flashes past.

WATER

Let us bless the humility of water,
always willing to take the shape
of whatever otherness holds it.

—John O'Donohue

Thirteen Skeins of Irish Knowing

—after Wallace Stevens

I

In emerald fields
braided haystacks, men
stagger in the wind.

II

A woman and wool thread
knit a home.
A woman and wool thread and blanket stitches
weave memories.

III

Like three chains,
the Trinity braids my life—
eternal knot.

IV

Fragments of tweed and old suits
patched into diamonds. Green grown
brown bodes hunger.
Braided knots and flour sacks
empty.

V

Black leaves curl in September mist.
Tragedy weaving roots.

VI

Fog spins low, thick,
frost braiding thatch, lake—
Ice Moon halos the night.
Curled in quilts, children witness
shadows swelling, their own hollow
eyes and bellies fill with winter white.

VII

Oh lonely women of Kilkieran,
where are all your children?
Do you not see how the gray in your braids,
your swollen bellies, blistered tongues
sent them searching the blood-dark sea?

VIII

I know the hush of midnight,
the song thrush greeting dawn.
I know, too,
the skein that weaves
families though acres of waves churn between them.

IX

She suffered the Atlantic,
her mam's quilt bearing
what was left of her dreams.

X

At the city's shore, she pinned up her braids
and left the boat. Dust and ash
slipped like a chain around her neck,
erasing the last traces of heather and tide.

XI

In Kentucky, a second cousin
faded into the mines,
the gloom too much like strangling,
rotting blossoms. Another voyage.
This time iron rails needled countryside,
Ohio sparked into view,
fabric of the river pricked by stars.

XII

The dress she wore on the journey
now cut for the baby, the quilt.

XIII

It misted all night, dawn
a moonstone over braided twigs.
Soon the sun would shine,
prisms stitched beneath
a gold and smoldering ring.

Born into Legend

We come to the coast—broken,
bruised—we reach the edge
of our world. Waves stretch, winds
shift—freedom in the West.

Waked, we want a different,
new beginning. Instead, death clings
like barnacles on our ships.
Anchored in murky holds, this damp womb
chokes us.

     We're birthed
through narrow stalls. We knot
in cages, pens—stench and sickness
dock at the harbor.

        Finally permitted
into cities, towns, we're strangers
among strangers. Kerchiefs swapped
for aprons, brogues swallowed in shame,
even God is different here.

What do we keep, what to abandon?
Tied to our past, memory beckons.
Nightmares from the Old Country blur
into dream. Ancient enemies—
hunger, poverty—they're here, too.

Orphans from that old world, our families
become rooted, grow in this one.
How many tides have turned since our fathers,
our mothers crossed the sea,

leaving behind an ocean of graves?

Taste of Salt

Seaweed snarls the crowded sky,
dark clouds looping like city smog.
Traffic rumbles, seething embers
urging a pause in breath. No sun,
no dazzle of blue to hinder, dissuade me.
Seams of sand and water blink away,
my eyes unravel, waves stretch.
Shells appear, disappear. Your absence
makes me the waiting one.

Curling surf imitates alpine wood smoke,
and empty cottages stun the gray, this house
but you withdraw. Raw February.
Dogs bark across the neighborhood,
street lights trace an acorn—
aimless, drifting the shoreline.
I knew you out of season.
Now I'm the stars—smoke in the night.

Between Sky and Sea

Clouds hang heavy above the swollen river.
Cragged granite juts over tumbling water—
briny tongue gulping silt, swirling rock.

Terns and cormorants shriek as rain whispers past.
Foam fizzes, seasons the shore
to mingle in pools of jade and teal.

Squeals from curlews, oystercatchers,
sand dense, speckled with kelp and broken coral,
shells sea-washed and shiny through the mizzle.

Trust this day, this hour—
memorize this moment, a softness unexpected,
when the world was not about you.

In Praise of Oceans—

white crests leaping for heaven
only to surge on shores with rock, with shell
to spume again and then retreat.
The heave and swell, peak and trough of salt
licking skin, crusted dry under sun,
shedding onto towels striped and damp.
Praise be to seaweed somersaulting through coral,
threadfin spied and gripped by gulls
laughing across the draughts.
Praise to molecules of hydrogen and oxygen spinning
across grains of sand roving coast to coast
by rivers' mouths, by marsh and mangrove,
from clouds blooming silver-gray over the horizon,
fog and mist smudging the sinking sun.

Ocean View

Scales sizzling in sun, she arches her back,
eyes damselflies harmonizing with salt breeze.
Outcrop of rock her sanctuary,
she lowers herself back into the tide, dizzy with heat
and half-blind from the mounting yellow globe.

Turtle grass climbs to a spit of sand.
Overhead a kingfisher screams, plunges
past periwinkle and apple snails
to pierce a fiddler crab sliding along the shallows.
Her webbed hands grip barnacles, she stretches
for one last gasp of air, fin twitching, then she's gone,
furling water into froth and fizz.

Written in Water

—Connemara, Ireland

Taste the ocean on your lips.
Wind scorns the sun, tosses
your hair till you can't see,
can only feel June's raw bite.
Foxglove curves on the cliffs,
purple bells summoning the dawn.
Moss dimples, water faeries
flirting in the spray.

Here, in the half-light, shadows dust
the stones and highlight fussing gulls,
conceal the rooks, their cawing demands.
Breathe the salt, the Burren
gray and hazy across the bay.
You can't remember the last time
you cried for beauty.

Two boys and a girl plunge onto the sand,
chase clouds, kelp that laces the shore.
Sprites vanish into tidal pools,
wind frothing the waves. Sun whispers
across the gathering blue, plovers
hopping in and out of the surf.
Rush and foam calling, calling.

Starlight Falling

Rain rinses honeysuckle and pear
   from late summer, hunger nudging
my dreams, giving them the voice of scent.
    Water lashes, roams the fields,
   nibbles edges of the road.
Sight fails, blurs hushed green
   as streams wash over stone, slip
over the mountainside, curving
    and bending into the ravine.
   Drenched cows and sheep plead.
Drizzle shifts to mist, fog.

The Wine Moon sings behind clouds.
    A swan nuzzles her cygnets on the bank
   while they poke at seeds swollen in mud.
Time scatters starspray, blossoms stripped,
    dappling the hedgerows, the river.
   They tumble over rock, clinging together,
harvesting pools of light.

I abandon you each night—

leave splintered sleep under
April's growing moon,
Hydra crystalling the heavens.
Air slips over my skin—this human skin
that flirts and feigns—
          to rush through pricking thistle,
                    heather purpling with perfume.
              Across the fringe of rocks I dance
                        on lilac sand where waves hush
                    the strand. A harem of heads etch
                              the darkness…

          Shock of amethyst sea greets my feet   my legs
                  tongues my thighs   my hips   breasts   neck
wavelets lick my face, white and plum whorls splashing
                  foam, salt into my eyes, dark eyes
          I thrust my head under,
                    velvet bodies encircle me   spinning
              with me, the tide   Whiskers tickle,
                  flippers stroking my skin, this skin…

          Pocked water mirrors the moon,
                    cratered, heavy. My lungs,
          two orchids insisting light, air.
                    The sand, the rocks, periwinkle dawn—
              surf whispers the shore,
Hydra faded to a hiss.
I cross the grass, the lavender
in this skin, your skin…

Three Sisters

—Dingle, County Kerry, Ireland

Waves spiral their last gasp onto shore.
Spray spills the air, effervesces. The peaks
of the Sisters sulk in the dawn, gulls nag.

Speckled seals waddle the margin
of sea and sand, wedge themselves
into rock pools, watch the swells.

Pink and yellow ribbon the sky,
unravel into blue that spreads
from the lip of sea, now a mirror.

Alone on the strand, I savor the day ahead.
Turning toward shore, I miss gray clouds
spooling in from the deep.

Leaving You in *An Fheothanach*

—Dingle, County Kerry, Ireland

Waves crest, staccato the rocky shore
then foam into nothingness.

Late summer rakes the timothy,
ridge shadowing horizon's edge.

Clouds scribble a hydrangea-blue sky,
sweep salty tang to the cows, the vetch.

Bruised with heat, forget-me-nots droop,
but one pink bud dares

the sun, and I bend to its sweetness.
At the heart, a ladybug

kisses my lips, ocean whispering
its secrets.

Pursued

A rip in the clouds, thunder swallowed
by lightning, and the rain breaks,
muscles its way to the ground.
Winds its way through rocks
to the river's crooked banks.

A fox barks from its burrow
and the air—the air suspends
in gray, fog and mist anchoring
the fields, masking the mountain tops
and shifting everything close—closer.

Lament

Mourning Moon veiled… unveiled…
veiled,
clouds scatter the sky.
Like a wolf devouring early snow after autumn's drought,
my thirst for you rages—wrestles
to fathom a soul broken, spilled out—
a shore lashed by seas,
pebbles and shells churning in the frenzied surge.
Straining to pierce the shadows' darkest depths,
stars thread a feeble light.
Desperate, they pulse and
fracture.

Breath of Our Words

Blanched hydrangeas nod bulbous heads
as wind screaks through branches,
the cost of poplar leaves under gray—
    grayer skies.
This morning I heard news
about a past president's death, wished
him God-speed as rain lashed
and spooled the windows.
    With December's wind wrapped close,
I relish the hearth, your hand on my thigh.
All maps guide us to a destination—else why look?
        Where am I headed today?

Sometimes the journey requires rest.
No need to add stones to the path—
    unless I pile them on the side,
shape a place to relax, to breathe lighter
as we set down our bags.
Take only what is necessary
                    the remainder of the way.

The Dark is Light Enough

Adder twisting in its grip,
a barred owl glides above fields
faded and stubbled
with cut stalks, empty husks.
Wings sigh the chill night
as the Storm Moon struggles to its height,
promise of snow in ash-colored clouds.
Wind-chimes echo far away,
a neighborhood dreaming
as ropes of rain slip between fissures of bark,
ice burning into veins of white.
Midwinter's curse—the core of the forest
frozen, waiting.

March Inventory, Ireland 2016

[A]n average of 1,150 migrants and refugees
arrived in Greece per day in mid-March.
—Danae Leivada

Moss breathing the shadows
of purple dawn
scales the oak, the alder,
urges bursts of leaflets
to lace the woods with spring.

> *Clouded in salt and sand, you rise*
> *from the Aegean Sea, fear and hope*
> *devouring the shards of your life.*
> *Skin and soul raw, you compass the beach,*
> *scour the waves for your daughter,*
> *her yellow dress seared into memory.*

Here, primrose and celandine scatter fields,
sun sculpting clouds into sea foam
at horizon's edge. Warblers, chiffchaff treble
the whitethorn, brambles scratching
the sky's wide gaze.

Ebb and Flow

Saplings shiver—March dripping
from thick woolen skies.
Fishermen lure the dawn,
water glossy, mist swimming
between mountains, into coves.

Here, where mockingbirds, sparrows chatter
and geese crackle the cattails,
man's absence delights.
Beneath the surface, brown-freckled scales
undulate, curve under boats,
ignoring the lines, the bait.

Shadows cast by our desires
dive deeper, into places we cannot follow.

In Praise of Snow Days

Waking to the perfect silence
of a muted world, gray stippled
by white on white—downy softness
with a shiver. Burrowed in blankets
and nuzzled in warmth, thoughts
of star frost and lavender shadows
lure me deeper into dreams.

Sitting with Wordsworth

—Grasmere, England

The lake slips unnoticed, hidden by houses
not there when you wrote, while water braids
strands off the slopes of Silver How, slap-dashing stones
as it falls. Tucked now into a side street, Dove Cottage snugs
a cluster of silver birches, the garden gorged
with primrose and speedwell, bees sipping the honeyed hours.

The path splits, rhododendron and daffodil winding
uphill toward the shelter you and your sister relished
in snow or rain, valeria breaching rock walls.
The weight of ink—two centuries' worth—saturates the air,
faint vibrations of language fragrant around me.

Pied wagtails, house martins chuff in tumbling clematis.
My breath falters while I scribble on this bench
where you invited Holly Blues and Gatekeepers to *stop here
whenever you are weary and rest as in a sanctuary.*
This angle reveals a bit of water combed by the breeze,
a boater paddling—the gift of a moment lingering with you.

Ocean Triptych

I.

Waves chant, whispering *te amo*, *te amo*,
foam rushing sand in Cocoa Beach, in Miami.
Pelicans arch ancient wings
over sun-streaked blue, shells ruffled,
wrapped in liquid warm and bright.

II.

Gulls tug sea mist from the Skelligs to Inis Mór—
dappled monochrome considering forgotten corners.
Sea pinks blush the cliffs, the tufts of green,
beehive huts polished with spray,
sheep hushed and watchful above the bay.

III.

California coast—mystery of rock and water—
froth spumes, soars—whirlpools eddy the sand.
Seaweed tossed and withering, shearwaters skim
teal and turquoise while fly fishers wait, wading
swirling edges. Salt stings, shells and broken glass
flashing through the shingle.

Released into the Blue

Late August, pears nod from branches
   thick and full. The river licks its banks,
      frogs deep-throating the reeds.
     Upstream, two girls squeal on a trestle,
swimsuits dry as they peek over the edge.

   Reclining under leafy shadows
I witness the courtship song of summer—
      boys circling midstream, urging
   the girls to join them, vouching for the depth,
    the warmth of the current.
Their vigil rewarded, the blonde tucks her elbows
       and leaps away from the pilings.

   Droplets crystal, scatter, and fracture.
The boys whoop as she emerges, vision fogged.
   Mia, come on, she calls the mute statue
    still gripping wooden planks.

  The air ripples with sound.
     Fear sparks the sunburned face—
visions of a train as unimaginable as quarks to a Neanderthal.
      Hectoring crows flap the tree line,
    ragweed dusting the river,
     and the trestle groans and grumbles.
The girl arcs over the water, reflection rising to catch her.

How the Rain Falls

Fog heavy over the riverbank,
cotton-thick, an echo of gray.
Solitude fastens its teeth,
and I ache from wounds that needle
my imagination and my nightmares.
Where did you go before you left?

Sweetgums creak and groan,
an oak sliding sideways in the woods.
Later the sun will thrive,
a wild blue scorching the mist
that wraps my skin
and soaks through bone
leaving the core of me cold,
frozen through fiery July days.

Thunder swells.
Rain drums down, now the only sound.
I watch love, wearing galoshes, walk away.

Medley of the Sea

—Staffa, Scotland

Sunlight chases heather across the moors
of Mull, clouds swirling legato blue.
Summer purples, thistle stitches the fields
with swift perfume,
slipper of moon chanting goodbye.

Over the water to Fingal's Cave,
anchor the boat and scramble to the top.
Kneel above the rocks.
Let breath cheat wind
and stare into the smashing murk,
panicked swells a counterpoint
to its still center.
Gannets and cormorants harmonize
the pulsing melody,
staccato boom of waves on rock.

On firefly nights, the cry of the snipe
shrieks with the measured sweep of sea.
Cavern rumbles and basalt froths,
memories of bards and warriors glisten,
crumble under cobwebbed fate,
pebbles churning the tide around pillars of stone,
hissing organ surging with spume.
Forte. Diminuendo.
Twilight pulses, echoes the moors
across the channel, mist cold and rising.

Invitation

—Isle of Skye, Scotland

Come to the Cuillins when gray drapes the horizon—
rain tapering to mist that dimples faerie pools.

Streams rush over rocks where moss softens stone,
splashes of green on this dingy day.

Wind funnels arches and grottos, gorse sunning hazel scrub.
Marguerites nod in ragged grass, mountains brooding behind.

A feather of movement—a flash then gone—
and you step into frosty water,

a song sighing through the lea. An Orange-Tip lingers
over thistle, wings quivering with joy.

Epilogue

Dark Coming Fast

Hawthorns curve the fields,
carved by air whisked from the sea.
Deep breaths of salt, of mown grass
flavor our tongues and throats—
whisper us back to the beginning:
                      earth, wind, water, fire.

The cliffs, scoured and worn, persist in silence,
wind sculpting ridges and hollows,
ocean rushing the shingled shore,
tide surging with the sun.

Here, where our fathers and grandmothers roamed,
we wait, clouds gathering like a shawl,
scorn the pace nature takes
as we brace against each moment
salt stings our cheeks, hair whipped wild.
We face the West, the sunset,
                      our own awakening.

Edge of the Echo

—after Amergin

I am the wren psalming the rising sun
I am the foam of the sea rushing the shore
I am the deer that leaps through woods,
I am the purple thistle, velvet and sting,
I am the otter romping the river,
I am the raindrop that sweetens the spring,
I am the red fox, tail brushing the field,
I am the moss that furs the bark of the oak,
I am the dolphin whistling in the waves
I am the hawthorn, berry and blossom, blush in the hedgerow,
I am the quicksilver moonbeam,
I am the center of the eye, pursuing the horizon,
I am the breath of God—stardust and song.

Notes

Pages 13 and 124: Amergin is an unknown bard or leader of the ancient Irish who composed the Song of Amergin; in Gaelic spelled *Amhairghin*

Page 18: *Día dhuit* is hello and *Día is Muire dhuit* is the return greeting of hello in Gaelic

Page 20: "Daisy a Day" by Jud Strunk

Page 24: Line by Lucille Clifton

Page 25: Imbolc is also known as Saint Brigid's Day (February 1) and marks the beginning of Spring

Page 33: Celtic goddess associated with war and fate, usually foretelling doom, death, or victory in battle

Page 34: With thanks to Robert Frost

Page 35: October 31, also known as Samhain when Celtic tradition says the souls of the departed return to earth

Page 36: An Irish saying

Page 38: *Petalouda* is Greek for butterfly or soul

Page 52: With thanks to David Whyte

Page 55: Line by Oscar Wilde

Page 56: Wyrt (or wort) is an Old English type of herb or root

Page 60: The men and women of Auvillar, France, have been known to write their burdens/troubles on slips of paper and toss them in the Garrone River to be taken far away

Page 61: Lines by TS Eliot, Geoffrey Chaucer, William Shakespeare, and Edna St Vincent Millay

Page 71: May 1, a celebration of the beginning of summer signifying the Celtic importance of fire (the return of the sun) and fertility, also known as Beltane

Page 74: Coomcallee is a mountain in Kerry, Ireland; *cum* means hollow; the Irish name of the place is *Com Caillí*

Page 77: Smoored is Scottish meaning to put out, smother, or suffocate

Page 78: This poem remembers those who died in the shootings of the mentioned cities in July 2015: Kate Steinle; Randall Smith, Thomas Sullivan, Squire "Skip" Wells, David Wyatt, Carson Holmquist; Jillian Johnson and Mayci Breaux

Page 79: *Shomerim* is Hebrew for guardians or keepers of the dead

Page 80: Some victims of the Holocaust were taken from the listed cities

Page 100: Mizzle is Irish for a misty drizzle of rain

Page 105: Selkies are the Seal Folk of Scottish tradition who could change from seal to human form by shedding their skin and back again

Page 115: Line from "To a Butterfly"

KB Ballentine received her MFA in Poetry from Lesley University, Cambridge, MA. She has participated in writing academies in the United States and Europe, and she holds graduate and undergraduate degrees in English.

She currently teaches high school theatre and English and adjuncts for a local college. She also conducts writing workshops throughout the United States.

Published in numerous literary journals and anthologies, KB was a finalist for the 2006 Joy Harjo Poetry Award and a 2007 finalist for the Ruth Stone Prize in Poetry. KB received the Dorothy Sargent Rosenberg Memorial Fund Award in 2006 and 2007. She was an Opera Omaha finalist in 2008, a 2014 finalist for the Ron Rash Poetry Award, and received the Libba Moore Gray Poetry Prize in 2016.

Learn more about KB Ballentine at www.kbballentine.com.

9 781604 542646